SHAMANISM
WHAT IT'S ALL ABOUT

Norman W. Wilson PhD

SHAMANISM
WHAT IT'S ALL ABOUT

Cover Design by

www.srwalkerdesigns.com

ACKNOWLEDGMENTS

Many thanks to Suzanne for being my devoted proofreader, soul mate, and photographer.

Stephen R Walker for his tireless efforts in cover design.

A special note of thanks goes to the librarians of the Sno-Isle Library System of Snohomish and Island Counties, Washington for their continued assistance in securing materials for my use.

Photographs from the collection of the United States Congressional Library.

Stuart Holland, my publisher, deserves special thanks for his tireless efforts on my behalf.

Elisapie for starting me on this long journey.

TABLE OF CONTENTS

INTRODUCTION

Some of the following information has been included in my novels. However, here, for the first time, I am sharing the rest of a special ceremony.

I met my first shaman when I was seven years old; actually, I was six with three months wait for number seven. My family and I were staying at an Indian campsite along the shores of the pristine Baskatong Reserve, a body of water and land that covered approximately one-hundred-sixty miles.

A personal and special incident remains embedded in my memory. The year was 1940.

It began one warm summer day in mid-July. My mother and I went into the forest to get our drinking water. Our log cabin had no inside plumbing so a daily trip to the natural spring was necessary. On the way back to our log cabin, she decided to stop at one of the teepees for a visit. Three women, one older than the other two, greeted us. We were invited to "sit a spell."

There was no furniture except for a three-legged stool. I sat on that, and my mother sat on folded animal skins. After a bit, the older woman pulled out a large knife and looked directly at me. I was sure I was about to be butchered and thrown into a huge pot that sat nearby in which something was cooking. I still remember its putrid smell. I stayed close to my mother.

The woman proceeded to pick up a sheet of white birch bark and with two very swift cuts with her over-sized knife cut out an image and handed it to me. I hesitated— but finally reached out to take whatever it was she wanted me to have.

As I did she said, "You won't appreciate this now, later you will."

I am sure she cackled.

It was a carving of a woman's leg. By the look on my mother's face, she was not too happy. I kept that bark carving well into my late teens. It was passed on to a nephew. As we stood up to leave, the old woman said we were to come back that evening. She would have something else for me.

All day, I wondered what she had for me and if we would go back to see her. Since I was the only child there, it was difficult for me to keep my mind off the special gift. As I recall, I pestered my parents about it until my father said, "Enough. You'll find out when you get there." At least, with that, I knew we were going back to the teepee. Finally, just at sunset, my father and mother and I walked up to the teepees.

As was the custom, we exchanged gifts. My parents gave the older woman a bottle of bourbon. My mother received a birch bark basket and my father an elk's tooth fastened to a strip of leather. For a time, I thought she had forgotten me. I was mistaken.

My gift turned out to be a handmade bow and two arrows. I am sure my eyes popped out of my head. She indicated I should follow her into the nearby woods. With an encouraging nod from my parents, I left with her. After a short walk, she stopped, placed an arrow in the bow and released it. I heard a slight rustle of leaves. She had shot and killed a grouse. She dipped the second arrow into the blood of the bird. She told me this was necessary to make the arrow fly true. She scooped up the dead bird and placed it in a leather sack and slung it over one shoulder. Once we returned to her teepee, the middle one of three, she told me to sit down by a fire pit.

She threw something into the smoldering fire pit, and it flamed up with a sudden swoosh. Slowly, she began to dance around the fire pit, and as she circled me, she began to chant. It sounded something like *he-ay-hee-ee*. I don't know what it meant. I felt a tingling sensation flow throughout my body. It was a magical moment.

When she stopped chanting and dancing she leaned over me, placed a bloody thumb on the center of my forehead and said, "Don't wash your face for three days."

I was delighted. I wouldn't have to wash my face and have my mother always scold, "wash behind those ears."

Was this a shamanic initiation? It was only the beginning. Did that make me a shaman? No. I would go through other "ceremonies" and spend many hours in the forested areas as well as open fields and fantastic shorelines. There, to learn plants. My journey to the Spirit World has been detailed in other books and sometimes changed for story-line effectiveness.

What follows is an attempt to bring about an understanding of what shamanism is all about.

PART ONE
GENERAL INFORMATION

Ten Bears' Last Spirit Quest
A digitized version of the original painting by
award-winning American artist, Gerald Roberts.

ORIGINS OF THE WORD SHAMAN

What is the origin of the word shaman (pronounced SHAYman or SHA-man)? There is some disagreement about the actual origin of the word. Some scholars claim the word shamanism is so indiscriminately used. It no longer has immediately identifiable meaning. The word pretty serves as another example as it is used in "It's a pretty day" or "That's a pretty dumb thing to do." And there are those who claim a complete definition is impossible. Two Dutch diplomats who accompanied Peter the Great's emissaries to China during the late Seventeenth Century are credited with first using the term, shaman.

In 1875, the Encyclopedia Britannica published an article by A.H. Sayee, which used the word *shaman*. Opinion indicates the word is of Tungas origin. More specifically, it appears that the term came from the Manchu-tangu dialect of Siberia, from where we derive our most common usage.

However, even this is not without challenge. Some ethnolinguists claim the word derives from the Chinese *scha-man*, while others claim it's from the Pali *schamana*, a term used for a Buddhist monk. There does appear to be common agreement that the word shaman came into modern language from the Sanskrit, *sramana*.

The word shamanism, which has been around since the 1600s has now become a heuristic term in Western Culture and refers to a man or woman who fills several roles within the culture. Specifically, two aspects of shamanism have gained popularity: physical and psychological healing.

SHAMANISM IS NOT A RELIGION

Predating organized religions, shamanism is unto itself, not a religion. Because shamans adhere to a belief of a direct connection between healing and the spiritual world, it is easy to equate it with a religion. A Shaman or shamanka (the female counterpart of shaman) act as an intermediary between the natural world and the spiritual world. Simply stated, a shaman is someone who walks between worlds.

**Figure 1 Goldes Shaman Priest
in his Regalia**

Despite some claims, shamanism is not a cult. Admittedly, there are those who have linked themselves in a cult-like fashion to some of the fundamental shamanic practices, particularly those from South America. It appears the interest is in the use of hallucinogenic drugs. It's doubtful if their use actually brings about an understanding of reality or the use of the individual's inner energy to heal anyone. One needs to beware of fakes and frauds while dealing with modern shamanism.

A shaman does commune with the spiritual world, and he does so for several reasons. Among these reasons, the primary one is to heal a sick soul. Other reasons include the reading of the future, asking for the success of specific endeavors, or to function as psychopomp. Whatever the shaman wishes to accomplish; he does so by connecting with the axis mundi to create a special relationship with the Spirits and in some instances, actually gains control over them. The *axis mundi* also called the cosmic axis, world axis, world pillar, center of the world, or world tree, in certain beliefs and philosophies, is the world center, or the connection between Heaven and Earth. Despite rumors and myth, generally speaking, a practitioner of shamanism is not involved in bringing about harm or 'evil' to someone.

Shamanism is not a specific set of beliefs inculcated in an organized uniform system throughout the world. It does not contain a dogma that outlines the steps in the adulation of a divinity. This does not mean there are not similarities. The primary similarity is the recognition of a spiritual world and the existence of Spirits. Specific ceremonies, chants, and training do not appear on a universal or worldly plane. Cultural differences are a singular mark.

WHAT IS CORE SHAMAISM?

Core Shamanism is a term introduced by world-famous anthropologist, the late Michael Harner, in the mid-1980s. The word core means the choicest or most essential or most vital part of some idea or experience. It is the applicable, basic and fundamental identifying terms used to describe. Simply put, core shamanism takes the best from traditional shamanic practices of aboriginal peoples and brings them into the modern world.

Appealing to people who are on quests for transcendence and healing, core shamanism offers the opportunity for direct contact with the Spirit World. What do transcendence and healing mean? Transcendence is a state of existence that has overcome the limitations of physical existence, and by some definitions, has become independent of it. It is journeying to another realm; perhaps to a parallel universe. Healing implies and incorporates both physical and psychological conditions of the human being.

A word of caution is appropriate now. When making contact with the Spirit World never do so in a frivolous or light-hearted manner. It does not exist for your entertainment! Don't approach the Spirit World with a litany of requests.

What does core shamanism advocate? First is the concept of journeying into alternate realities. Using hallucinogens such as Datura, yopo, peyote, or ayahuasca creates an altered state of consciousness conducive to traveling to different realms. These mind-altering drugs are not the preferred method of journeying and if one chooses to use them, he should be very careful. The recommended and most widely used method for journeying is drumming. Drumming alters the natural vibrational levels of the body and brain.

In addition to traveling to different realms, core shamanism has seven major principles.

1. Sentience and interconnectedness exist throughout the cosmos. Humankind has long believed there is a living universe; that all things are alive. Animism is the label. Sentience goes further than this. Within sentience, there is the belief that all things are connected much as in the old song, "the hip bone connected to the knee bone." After all, we are made of the dust of the stars. Probably, the best illustration of this is the story of the butterfly that flaps its wings in China, and the repercussion flows throughout the world. It's the classic example of the sensitive dependence on initial conditions in a deterministic nonlinear system. Despite modern science's claim to have found the "God Particle," they have not determined that which created it. In shamanism, there is no need for that because, for them, the cosmos is a living, creating entity.

2. There are two realities: ordinary material reality, that is waking life, and non-ordinary reality, populated by spirits, souls of the dead, deities, and transcendent powers. Do not assume non-ordinary reality is not real or that one is not fully aware of activity. Spirits generally appear during darkness. Some, however, do make themselves visible during daylight hours. Souls of the dead create some concern here because there are those who believe we do not die, but simply move on to a new life—born again, so to speak. Look at it this way, when one is born, he or she comes out of a dark, warm, comfortable world of the womb into an unknown bright, often chilly and uncertain new world. Some come without much struggle. Others have a difficult time. What we ordinarily call death is leaving the earth womb for another world. This other world is often

called the Akasha Record or Field, the place to which all energy returns to await future need and use. I simply say the soul returns to its source of creation.

This is not unusual. In the natural world, we find animals return to their place of conception. In the Northwest of the United States, where I live, salmon return to their place of birth to spawn. If we accept humankind as a part of the natural world, then such an idea is neither revolutionary nor unacceptable.

3. Realty is composed of three layers: Middle World (where we are now), Lower World, and the Upper World where spirit-teachers and animal spirits exist. Philosophers arguing for hundreds of years have not provided any clearer concept of reality than that found in core shamanism. Middle world, our current existence, does have spirits. They come into this world to help, to protect, and to heal. They remain here as long as their assigned tasks are not completed. The Lower World is the home of the power animals, and these may be normal animals such as birds, fish, bears, wolves, or they may be mythological animals such as the unicorn. Most shaman have a power animal that serves as a guide and guardian.

4. Reality is dualistic in that spirit and matter are distinct and are viewed as such. The issue of dualism has long plagued westerners. The shaman doesn't bog down in the issue. Spirit is and matter is. Man is a dualistic being composed of spirit and matter. This does not imply that they are diametrically opposed to one another. Opposite yes; opposed no.

5. It emphasizes helping and protecting others as well as one's self. The major function of the shaman is to help others get well physically and spiritually. For those of you, who might seek the help of a shaman don't ask him or her to help your favorite team to win the Nationals. In doing so, you also are asking for a

loser to be created as well. That's counterproductive. And don't ask to win the Lotto.

6. Alternate reality can affect material reality. Because this is near the end of the list, it does not lessen its importance. Journeying into alternate realities affects a change in material reality. It is here that future events may be changed.

7. Knowledge and direction come from the spirits. Knowledge about healing, and the directing that healing is to take comes from the spirit world. As the shaman journeys to another reality, dimension, or parallel universe, he or she goes with one specific goal in mind: what is he or she to do to help the client? Knowledge about the workings of the universe and humankind's relationship to that universe comes from the spirit world.

In core shamanism, the shaman travels to these other realities in an altered state of consciousness. The spirit world quest is focused. To help him or her achieve this altered state of consciousness, drumming is used rather than hallucinogens. Its methodical, steady beat (slightly over 200 beats per minute) changes the brain's theta, and alpha waves, that is, the telencephalic neurons are stimulated, and with 100 billion neurons and 100 trillion synapses in the brain, it can do whatever it desires.

FOUR TYPES OF SHAMAN

Despite the image of the shaman created by Hollywood and certain national magazines of a half-naked man with a painted face, clothed in animal skins, a shaman may be a man or woman and in today's world, more often than not, be dressed in a plaid shirt and blue jeans.

Admittedly, as the types of shaman are identified, there will be those who call such distinction splitting hairs. There is a simple reason for making these differentiations, and that is to bring about understanding. All shamanic practitioners do have two things in common—they all journey or travel to other realms, and they all seek the help and guidance from those that inhabit the spirit world.

The first type of shaman is the Healer. Healers journey to the upper and lower worlds to seek help to heal a sick person. The Healer also uses various remedies based upon natural plants and herbs. Salves, poultices, ointments, teas are made from plant leaves, berries, and roots of specific vegetation. Some of these remedies are short-term while others are for longer periods of time if they are to be effective. An example of a short-term remedy is bearberry for diarrhea, and Echinacea serves as an example for a longer-term remedy since it is used for the immune system. Warning: Do not attempt to use these without consultation with a shaman and or your medical practitioner. Crystals may also be used in the client's treatment.

The second type of shaman is the Soul Retriever. The Soul Retriever journeys to the other world to gather up a soul or part of a soul and return it to its source. Often, the shaman will have a spirit helper or guide for this undertaking. The client may have had his soul stolen by a hoodoo, an evil spirit. More will be said about the soul and soul retrieval in another section.

The third type of shaman is the Spiritual Healer. In today's world psychologists, psychiatrists, and counselors deal with emotional aspects of a person's life. The Spiritual healer does the same thing. He or she deals with anger, frustration, jealously, hate, prejudice, or self-defamation. Herbals, as well as music, is a part of the treatment. The client may be put in a modified hypnotic state. The shaman may go into a trance. During this trance state, the shaman may remove entities from the suffering person. The Spiritual Healer generally requires several sessions with a client.

The fourth type of shaman is the Messenger. The Messenger brings information back from the non-ordinary world to the world commonly called the real world. The messages may deal with immediate events or may predict those to come. These messages guide or direct individuals. In past years, the messages dealt with the hunt, crops, or a tribal move. The message can and may deal with all of humanity. The author's shamanic friend who lived in the Amazon jungle for eleven years of intense training is a Messenger for all of humanity.

Please understand an individual shaman may fulfill all four of these types or any combination of them. Whatever the role they take on, they all rely on their connection to the Spirit World.

WHAT A SHAMAN KNOWS

Shaman operate with a basic premise: The world is composed of invisible forces and/or spirits that affect all life—human and non-human. Resting within this premise is the notion that plants, rivers, lakes, oceans, trees, and rocks have their own special qualities. Modern science tells us there are forces, invisible to the naked eye. Consequently, the idea that certain individuals can tune into to these forces should not be shocking.

A shaman is not trying to prove rationality is unachievable; nor is he or she trying to prove that human belief systems not only determine our world but confirm it. For him, all things are possible. The shaman knows how to tap into universal consciousness, and because he does, he often functions as a healer. In some cases, he heals a whole community. In other instances, he brings harmony between man and nature and at other times between man and his fellow humans on an individual basis. To achieve this, the shaman knows how to retire into an altered state of consciousness. In some cultures, individuals use a variety of drugs to induce the shamanic state. I am opposed to such use. Grave permanent dangers lurk for the novice. There are other ways a shaman may create an altered state of consciousness; for example, by using sounds. Drums, flutes, humming, rattles are successful aids in helping a shaman reach an altered state of consciousness. Today, audio tapes, CD, DVDs are available to help project one into an altered state. These rely upon binaural beats to alter one's brain waves. The repletion of the sound OHM is a popular choice.

The shaman knows he must go into his altered state with a single question in mind, not a shopping list.

If he goes with such a list, disappointment will be the result.

The practicing shaman knows there are three levels in the shamanic world. These levels are not religious based. The first level of the shamanic journey is the *underworld*. At this level, emotions, memories, and psychic healing take place. Sometimes one encounters his power animal. Generally, access to the underworld is achieved by going through a tunnel (as did Enkidu in the Sumerian myth of Gilgamesh), or flowing down an underground river. Other times, one may achieve this level through a sudden flash or rappelling.

The second level is the *middle world*. Here plant spirits, spells, curses, and ghosts are located just outside of ordinary reality. The popular television series, Ghost Whisperer took place at this level. The shaman may seek an answer to his or her question or may be able to determine if he is headed in the right direction to find his requested solution.

The *upper world* is the third level of the shamanic world. Here, spiritual teachers and Jung's archetypes exist. The teacher arrives unbidden quite often and at first experience, may not be recognized. This third level requires extensive meditation and the production of an altered state. The shaman knows how to do this. Native American musicians David and Steven Gordon, Carlos Nakai, the Native Flute Ensemble or Scott August certainly would help set the tone for such meditation. Listen and let their song carry you. The harmonics are surreal.

A shaman is a sensitive and knows, intuitively what someone is feeling. He accepts his intuition's validity, and connects into the psychic and emotional energy of a person who has issues.

A cautionary word is essential in view of the Arizona sweat lodge tragedy. Beware of the self-proclaimed. It's good policy to know your guide. The shamanic state is not for everyone. Massive spiritual cleansing and renewal are not for everyone. A shaman, by whatever name you wish to call him, is not a catholicon.

THE SHAMANIC VIEW OF THE SOUL AND SPIRIT

One of the more difficult words to define is *soul*. It is one of those words that entered the main stream of thought, and as it did so, it lost much of its original intent as *the breath of life*.

Today we have Soul-mate, Soul-sister, Soul-music, Soul-train, and Soul-food. The word describes the sound post of a violin as well as the bore of a cannon. There are soul and body lashings, soul-candles, and soul-catchers. And let's not forget soul-ale. And then there are the expressions, such as he's a lost soul or a poor soul.

Figure 2 Hatali Nez, Navajo Shaman.

Spirit has just as many disparate uses. We talk about school spirit, team spirit, national spirit, company spirit, unclean spirit, the Holy Spirit, the spirit of cooperation, and the human spirit. Expressions like his spirit are broken, that is a mean-spirited thing to do, winning spirit, or get into the spirit of things, continue to show the mixed usage.

For the shaman, there is a decided distinction between soul and spirit. In the shamanic world, spirt also differs from Spirits. Spirit is the élan; whereas, Spirits are entities unto themselves. Briefly, the soul is that part of the human that is alive and manifests in the consciousness of the individual. It is that aspect of the human that defines individuality. And like the individual, it grows, learns, and changes. It is present upon the conception of the human being and upon the death of the physical body; it seeks to return to whence it came, the source of creation as I said earlier.

The shaman understands this mobility of the soul and when it becomes ill, stolen, or corrupted by an evil entity, the human spirit withers, and dissolves. Thus, the shaman is bound to mind-travel through an altered state of consciousness to non-ordinary reality, to locate the suffering soul, seek out a solution for its suffering, performs the necessary tasks of bringing health to the soul, and returns it so the physical body can become well.

MORE ABOUT SPIRIT, SOUL AND SHAMANIC BELIEFS

Modern science does not admit spirits exist. The medical world does not acknowledge the existence of the soul. Even so, both agree that there are some things they cannot explain, at least not at this time. However, one cannot say spirits and soul does not exist with absolute certainty.

We know thought exists; however, it has no shape, size, or weight. Is it any different from spirit or soul? Can a common ground for these two words be realized?

For those of you, who are religious history buffs, it can be said with certainty, most religions acknowledge the existence of a spirit-filled world. A very brief examination of the world religious ritual will reveal some interesting similarities. A short list would include the use of candles, incense, some form of music, monotonous repetitive chanting. Notice the subdued lighting in churches, synagogues, temples, and mosques and the play of color through stained-glass windows. Are not many of the rituals associated with religion representational of magical acts?

Spirit is over used as are such words as absolutely, exactly, great, and fantastic. For our purposes here, spirit has two meanings: First, those entities which exit outside of normal reality—supernatural. Second, it shall be used to reference that essence constituting all life forms; that is, that animating or vital principle held to give life to physical organisms.

Soul is the incorporeal essence that lives in a human body or any other living thing. This means that the soul is without the nature of a body or substance. One is a soul that has a body. Most cultures believe in an incorporeal realm, and this is particularly true for the shaman. When soulness is recognized in all objects that belief system is called animism, that is, all objects (stones, trees, plants, rivers, mountains) contain some form of a life principle.

For the shaman of old as well as those in our modern world, the belief that all things contain a living essence is sacrosanct. It is this fundamental belief that is responsible for the shaman insisting upon respect for all aspects of the natural and spirit worlds.

COLUMNA CERULUI AND SHAMANISM

An aspect of the world view requires further explanation. This is the shamanic relationship to the Columna Cerului.

Often called the Tree of Life or The Tree of Knowledge as found in Judaism and early Christianity or it may be the central axis of the cosmos or the Columna Cerului. Columna Cerului is the center of that which is and as such; it holds an importance in many ancient cultures. The idea, however, existed in most cultures since humankind became acculturated. Probably the earliest known record of the concept comes to us from the Ancient Egyptians' story of Osiris or more likely the works of Hermes Trismegistus collectively known as The Hermetica.

In contemporary times, actually a carryover from Medieval Europe, it is seen as the symbol used for the medical profession, the Asclepius Staff.

In shamanism, it is the shaman's staff that represents the Columna Cerului, and it is used to connect the three realms of the world: The Upper World, the Middle World, and third, The Lower World.

For the shaman, the Upper World is the world of the unseen in which there is potential waiting to manifest. The Middle World is the spirit aspect of the material world and is most like ordinary reality. The Lower World houses the spirits of animals, spirit guides, and of course, the human spirit after it leaves the physical body.

Because the staff is a representation of the Columna Cerului, it is a power tool, it is held in great respect, and it is treated with care. For the shaman, the Columna Cerului poses a definite paradox. For the shaman, the center of the world is everywhere. In his altered state of consciousness, the shaman physically remains firmly planted in the ordinary world but spiritually travels in non-ordinary reality. While in this trance state, the Columna Cerului becomes the spot upon which the shaman stands or sits and thus, becomes the center of the universe.

SHAMAN, SAGE, RACONTEUR

Figure 3 The White Singer

The shaman is a healer. He or she commands a local knowledge of medicinal herbs and plants, as well as the application of those to the sick. He treats everything from an upset stomach to menstruation issues to birthing pains. Often a journey to the Spirit World is required to determine the cause and potential cure for a client's disease.

The sage is not necessarily a shaman. Generally, he or she is the keeper of tribal wisdom. He provides the tribe and other seekers his advice on issues of governance, marriage, child-bearing, and rearing of children.

The raconteur, sometimes called the singer, is the story teller. He recounts in word or song, and or in dance, the history of his people, their battles, their tragedies, sacrifices, and sorrows. He tells the story of his people's creation and their relationship to the divine. Basically, he is a historian who preserves tribal culture. Most of the time the history is revealed only in the oral tradition. With the advent of modern recording tools, the role of the raconteur has changed. The shaman may encompass the role of sage and raconteur. Depending on the culture, the shaman's role may be expansive or narrowed to a specialization. He may function as a psychopomp and at other times, he may function as a communicator with only certain types of Spirits: animals, plants, water, heavenly bodies, or deceased humans. Whatever the role, be it shaman, sage, or raconteur, all are highly respected and are powerful members of the community. In the photo at the right, do you think this story teller is talking about a great buffalo hunt? Or is he talking about the fish that got away?

Figure 4 Raconteur

WHAT A SHAMAN DOES

Figure 5 Giving of the Medicine: The Sweat Bath

The word shaman conjures up images of half-naked wild aboriginals dancing around an open fire. Others imagine witchdoctors with hideous masks or painted faces, or voodoo doctors doing nasty things, or drugged up glazed hallucinating chanting figures, calling upon the

Spirits from the nether world. They are just as illusionary as the late movie star, Jeff Chandler playing Cochise.

A shaman has so much more to give than these illusionary phantasmagorias would have you believe. Some anthropologists and ethnologists have classified shamanism as an archaic-magical-religious phenomenon in which the shaman is a great master of ecstasy. This is not really a fair statement of what a shaman does. People who adhere to shamanic principles are not participating in a religion. They do not come together to worship a divinity.

What then does the shaman do? He creates an emotional state, an altered state of consciousness. True, some aboriginals in South America, as well as North America, use drugs to create the ecstatic state. As I have said before that is not necessary. Numerous other things are useful in creating an altered state of consciousness. The shaman has at his command flutes, drums, rattles, the dance, fasting, and meditation. He may use his own voice to enter a trance.

A shaman attempts to reintroduce harmony among the body, mind, and soul of his clients. He performs a wide variety of ceremonies, each with a different use in healing.

A specific rich background in medicinal plants and herbs and their uses add more to the shaman's arsenal of healing techniques. It is interesting to note there is now a physicians' desk reference book for herbal medicines. (See References)

NATIVE AMERICAN MEDICINE

In 1926, Jan C. Smuts introduced Holism. Such an approach is not new. For centuries, ancient Chinese traditional medicine, as well as that of the Indian Ayurveda, have treated the ill from a holistic point of view. Since the 1970's trends in contemporary medicine have continued to suggest a holistic approach to client treatment.

Native Americans have long placed an emphasis on the treatment of the whole person; that is, the body, mind, and spirit.

A key ingredient of Native American medicine is the belief that one's health inextricably connects to that individual's surroundings. Consequently, the shaman works to promote harmony between the body, mind, and spirit as well as harmony within the community, the environment, and the spiritual world.

There are four practices common to nearly all shaman.

1. Use of herbal remedies
2. Purging and or extraction
3. Ceremonies of purification
4. Contact with the spiritual world

Using herbs in cooking is nothing new but today many people are returning to an age-old practice of using herbal remedies for everything from emotional issues to skin problems, to hair restoration. Early humankind relied upon those herbs found in their local environments. From a wide variety of herbs, the shaman crates teas, broths, ointments, poultices, and salves to bring healing to his or her clients.

Purging and extracting involve the use of an herbal as a laxative as well as cathartic whereas extraction may involve the removal of an "evil spirt" or a piece of a stolen soul from a client.

Ceremonies of purification come into play once there has been an extraction. One of my favorite statements about sweat lodge purification comes from Cree medicine man, William J. Walk-Sacred: "When you come out of a purification lodge you don't feel the same as when you come out of a sauna. The ceremony is a rebirthing process." [F1] One's intention is crucial here. Entering a purification ceremony is not party time or something one does to be avant-garde.

Contacting the spiritual world is not to be viewed as a last resort. It is one tool among many; the shaman can call upon to help his or her client. One goes to the Spirit World for a specific reason. A shaman goes there to find an answer to a healing question, to get instruction for events, and to retrieve a soul or parts of a soul. Contacting the Spirit World should never be used as a parlor game.

The role of the shaman in these four practices is generally to function as an intermediary between the world of realty and the Spirit World. Today, many of the practices carried on by healers are working their way through modern medical practice as alternative medicine, a term I dislike. For the Native American, there is a strong belief that all things in nature are connected and that every human and non-human have a corresponding connection in the world of spirits. More importantly, they believe these spirits can help maintain and promote a return to good health.

Directly related to the concept that all things are connected is the Medicine Wheel. At the simplest level, a medicine well is a stone circle used for religious and healing purposes. In days gone by the circle was built on the ground. Pictured below is an ancient Medicine Wheel located in Wyoming [F2].

Figure 6 Medicine Wheel

Many users of earthen and stone wheels maintain there is a direct connection to earth energy and since the earth is a living organism such a notion is not unreasonable. Prayers and tobacco are offered at each of the four corners. Some shaman may add two additional directions: Up and Below. Colorful ribbons are frequently added to the prayer wheel announcing the purpose of the ceremony.

Today, temporary medicine wheels are created for special ceremonies and for healing procedures. I have created a small stone Medicine Wheel using crystals. One may create a small earthen Medicine Wheel in an office setting by building a small sand box, fill it with sand, and install crystals or stones, place wooden pegs around its outer edge.

Drawing on earth energy is a universal concept. There are many adaptations of the Medicine Wheel. In the yoga classes I take, my teacher has us lay down in a circle, heads pointed into the center, feet spread outward and slightly touching as we seek restorative and healing energy from the universe.

In addition to the Wyoming Medicine Wheel, there are others located in South Dakota, Colorado, Arizona, Oklahoma, and Iowa.

SHAMAN AS HEALER

Figure 7 Old Indian Witch Doctor

Healing is certainly one of the more important tasks of a shaman, if not the most important. In addition to healing, a shaman may ask the Spirits for a good crop, or he may conduct

special ceremonies, read the future, or interpret certain natural events.

In his medicine bag, the shaman has a vast knowledge of healing herbs and other plants. Among these, he would certainly include the following:

The shamanic healer will attempt to restore an individual's personal energy. The old adage, *mind over matter* certainly applies to a good deal of what the shaman does. The implication is a simple one, at least on the surface. The body can do much to heal itself.

Michael Harner in his *The Way of the Shaman,* tells us shamanism is an ancient methodological system of mind-body healing. There are numerous examples available today of mind-body healing. Often they are called miracles.

If the nature of the person's illness is serious enough, the shaman may go into an altered state of consciousness. In the trance state, the shaman works to restore the client's personal power or energy. He attempts this by direct communication with the Spirit World.

In this altered state, he hears, sees, and feels the presence of other entities. It is within this very special framework that the shaman seeks help for his client. He may have with him a spirit guide. This may be an animal or the soul of a deceased person. Together, they seek an answer to the client's illness. Upon his return to the ordinary world, the shaman may then perform any number of special ceremonies. These might include spiritual cleansing, extraction, or physical cleansing. If it is a spiritual issue for the client, the shaman will act accordingly.

PART TWO
TOOLS OF THE TRADE

THE SHAMAN AND DRUMMING

The drum plays a significant role for the shaman. The drum helps him move from ordinary reality to non-ordinary reality; a reality that is stilled filled with sights, sounds, feelings, and smells. And sometimes it is filled with unpleasant things; even soul searing things.

Besides the rattle, the drum is the instrument of choice for the healer and it varies in size. The drum is made of natural materials; wood, animal skin, and dyes from various plants. They may have an abstract design representing an animal spirit or totem. Often, the shaman will have a drummer rather than do the drumming himself.

Figure 8 Nunivak Drummer

Having a drummer allows the shaman to dance or perform other healing activities for his client.

With the steady monotonous beat of a skin drum, the shaman enters what the Australian Aboriginals call dreamtime. In today's world, this shift, in reality, is called a shamanic journey.

Because the shaman is highly intuitive, he tunes into the repetitive, monotonous beat of the drum, as he travels to commune with those who inhibit the ether world.

Once in dreamtime, the practiced shaman can go anywhere on earth, into the earth, into the heavens, and from one universe to another. He mind-walks these areas with complete ease. The beat of the drum is the vehicle through which the shaman achieves dreamtime.

Drumming brings the shaman's rhythm and personal resonance into sync with the natural world, that is, the actual physical beat of the Earth herself, and most certainly, with the universe, both of which have sounds and vibrations of their own.

The implied therapeutic value of shamanic drumming is enjoying a resurgence. Parlayed as being helpful, drumming's uses include the reduction of stress, the lowering of blood pressure, the reduction of muscular aches and pains and illness, both physical and psychological. [F3]

In spite of the renewed interest in drumming as a therapeutic tool, it has been around for thousands of years, used by shaman in every culture as a tool to alter the state of consciousness and not necessarily as a device for the improvement of health. Any consideration of using drumming as a healing device requires further study. The vibration of the drumming may have an impact on the energy level of the body.

THE SHAMAN'S MEDICINE BAG

Figure 9 Medicine Bags

There are two general types of medicine bags used by practicing shaman. Both are highly personal and reflect the shaman's knowledge and skills.

The first bag is a small leather pouch attached to a leather string and worn around the neck. It may or may not have decorations. If the person is a shamanka, the medicine pouch may have beads and fringe. This leather pouch is a power pouch; that is, it is a source of the energy and power of the shaman or shamanka. It may contain a bear claw; earth warmed small stones, the bones of a spirit animal, perhaps a crystal or two. It is sacrosanct. The second pouch, also made of leather, may or may not have beaded decorations. Some may have a symbol created with vegetable dye. The symbol would be representative of power animals, plants, spirit, or spirit figures. The bag may also contain a ceremonial mask and rattle, various herbs and medicinal plants, totems, tobacco, and ground cornmeal. This is equivalent to the old-fashioned black satchel doctors used to carry. It contains the tools of the trade and because of its size; the shaman carries it over his shoulder. Additionally, the shaman has a smaller bag he may carry around his neck or on a hip. It may contain plant leaves for the making of teas.

The shaman uses his medicines to ward off evil, to get rid of negativity inhibiting a client, to disperse anger, hatred, and depression. Items would include special charms (totems) to attract good luck, happiness, prosperity, and if needed, love. To appease a disgruntled spirit, the shaman spreads cornmeal around his client.

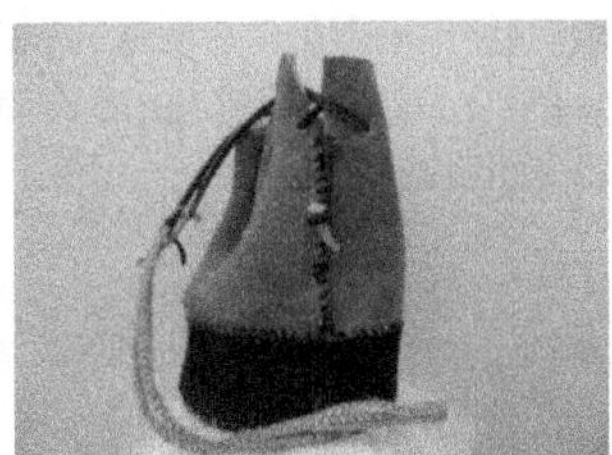

Figure 10 Small Medicine Bag

Finally, the medicine bag might also contain natural substances to cause a flame to flare up or to create a large amount of smoke so the shaman could disappear and return with a different mask, for example.

RATTLES

If the shaman doesn't use drums to help him enter an altered state of consciousness, he may use rattles. As with the drumming, he may have others do the rattling.

The purpose of the rattles, as it is with the drums, is to create a hypnotic rhythmic pattern. A practiced shaman will not require an extensive use of the rattles.

The rattles may be decorated with animal or plant symbols, feathers, beads. and may also have clamshells, pine cones, or horse chestnuts that function as bells. Additionally, and depending upon the skill of the maker, the rattles may be in the shape of an animal—an abstraction; nevertheless, the shapes are still recognizable.

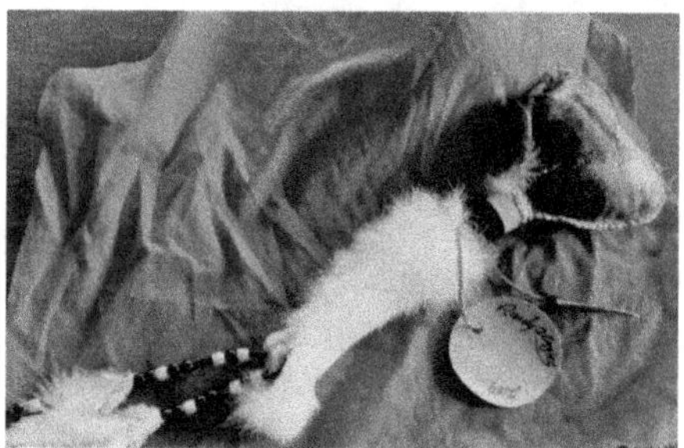

Figure 11 Rattle

To create rattles, the shaman might use gourds, carved wood, or dried thrush and animal skins. Once the gourd is dried, the shaman may insert additional seeds or small pebbles to create more sound. For ease of use, the shaman may insert a wooden handle at the end of the gourd. The rattle shown in Figure 10 was made for me by Randy Two-Eagles Billings and is made of deer skin. It's subtle sound is very effective.

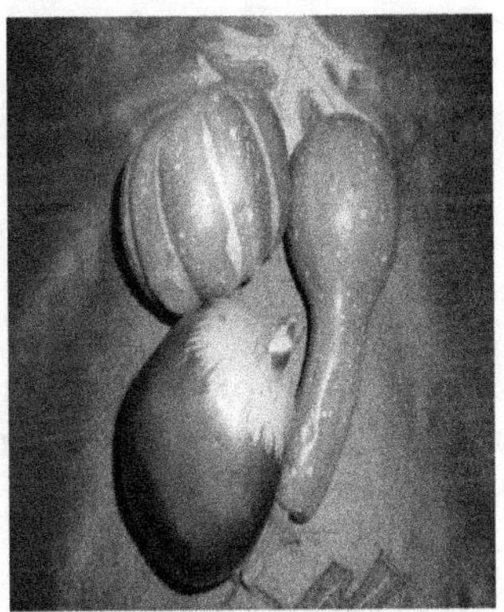

Figure 12 Gourds

In addition to using hand rattles, the shaman may have small rattles tied to his or her feet. This is done to help emphasize the rhythm while the shaman dances around the client. The purpose of such rhythmic sounds is to change the client's energy vibration and to help eliminate what we now call blockages

SMUDGING

A person, house, animal or any objects may be smudged. The purpose of the smudge is to get rid of negativity, that is negative energy or spirits. Two approaches to smudging for healing are in keeping with our focus. A smudge stick may be the simplest to use. It's a stick of cedar or Palo Santo.

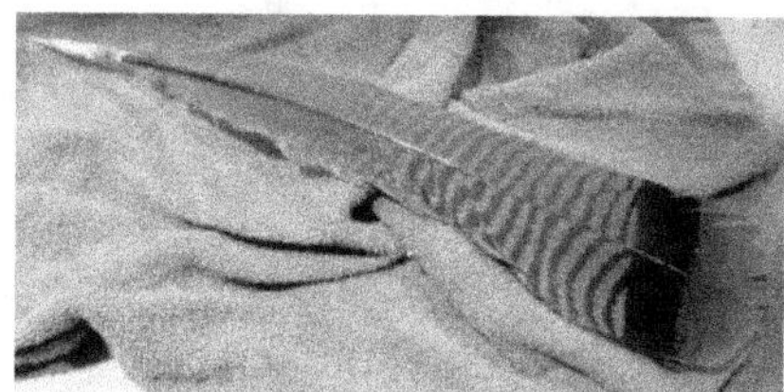

Figure 13 Smudge Fan

Palo Santo, one of my favorites, is an excellent wood to use. It comes from a tree, often described as magical that grows along the South American coast. Many view the Palo Santo tree as holy. Harvesting is not done until the tree has died. Sticks are available at many shops. Its odor is not as pungent as sage. It is an excellent choice for those who have an aversion to sage.

Light one end of the Palo Santo stick, gently blow out the flame and then waft the smoke around the individual being smudged or walk through a house or building. If an individual is to be smudged, a smudging fan is used to direct the smoke to various parts of the individual's body.

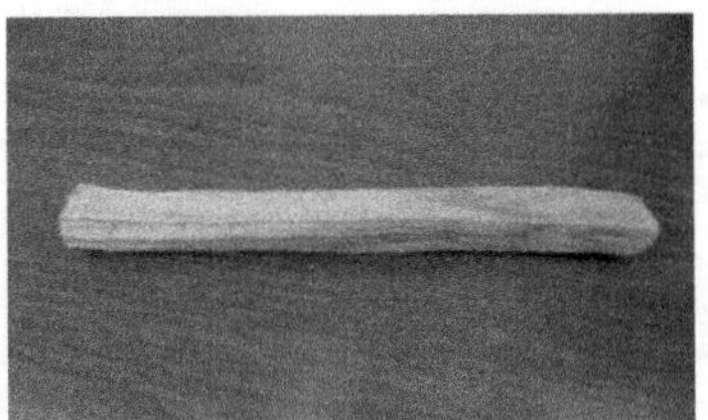
Figure 14 Palo Santo Stick

A second approach a shaman may use generally calls for a sage bundle. Once it has been lighted, and flames blew out, the shaman fans the smoke to each of the four directions, and as he does, he calls upon the Spirits offering a prayer to each. Upon completion of the homage to the four directions, the shaman then fans the sage smoke around the client, house, or object. The smoke is wafted from the bottom of the client's feet to the top of his or her head and then back down again. The smudging should be around the whole body.

Figure 15 Sage Bundle

A third technique for smudging includes the use of a sea shell in which a mixture of sage, Palo Santo and copal is then lighted. If a large enough seashell is not available any small dish that can withstand heat is usable. There are several kinds of sage. I prefer white sage and it is grown in the wild. Drying time for bundles depends upon the local and regional climate.

THE SHAMAN'S STAFF

Figure 16 Shaman's Staff

One of the major tools available for a shaman's use is a staff. For the shaman, it is *amitai*, that is, it is alive. The staff is usually made of maple or oak and may have ornamentation such as caved totems, rawhide strung with beads, quills, sacred animal bones, feathers, and in some cases they may have *hanhinuur* attached. These cones create a noise when shaken, thus making the staff a rattle.

It is believed the staff makes it possible to increase spiritual power for the shaman. As such, the staff contains *ezetei* or a master spirit. The staff then, is a connection to the three realms: Upper, Middle, and Lower, thus allowing him to access the worlds of his ancestral spirits.

The shaman uses his staff to stomp the ground around an ill person to chase away an evil spirit or demon. He also uses it to call his spiritual helper. There are many written examples of the staff as a power tool. Two come to mind; Moses of the Old Testament and of course from King Arthur, the marvelous Merlin.

Perhaps the singular connection of shaman's staff is its apparent relationship to the World Tree or the Tree of Life. It is a symbol embedded in mythology, religion, and science. It is in the literature of Ancient Egypt, Assyria, and China. It's in Baha'i, Judaism, Christianity, Hinduism, and Mormonism. Without much effort, one may view the Columna Cerului as a universal and for the shaman, it is a universal connection to all that is, has been, or will be.

The staff shown in Figure 16 was made for me by Bill Paulson. The crow, hand carved from hemlock, symbolizes life's magic, intelligence, and flexibility. Not shown in the photo is a long leather strap with red and yellow beads and white feathers.

THE DANCE

Figure 17 Sia Buffalo Dancer

The dance, matter its origin, plays a significant role in all cultures. Evidence exists of the dance in prehistoric times. It may predate humankind's use of fire. No matter its form, the dance supported by the rhythmic pattern laid down by the drummer, is a vital part of all Native cultures and especially early Native American Culture. The dancer accompanies the beat of the drummer with rattles and with his feet. In some instances, rattles are attached to the ankles of the dancer.

In by-gone years, there were many reasons for the dance. Among those were blessings for a good harvest, a successful hunt, for rain, and a variety of initiation ceremonies. It was an instrument for healing or encouraging affairs of the heart.

The rhythmic overlay of the drum and rattles echoes the natural beat of the universe, and the creation of that beat is reflected in the movements of the dancer.

When the shaman dances, he does so to chase out an evil spirit that inhabits a sick person or to create a special prayer.

During the dance, the shaman wears a specific regalia, including a headdress and other significant adornments. He may have rattles tied to his ankles.

The shaman uses the dance as a conduit for creating an altered state of consciousness. During this state, he travels to the Spirit world to seek an answer to his question—usually related to a way to help his client.

The dance and all its magic is an expression of the rhythmic harmony between man, nature, the universe and the Spirit World. The whole imagery is one of rhythmic flow and beauty.

PART THREE
MEDICINALS AND HERBS

57

THE SHAMAN AND HIS MEDICINE

Since the 1970s, trends in contemporary medicine have continued to suggest a holistic approach to client treatment. However, that idea was not new. In 1926, Jan C. Smuts introduced Holism. Holism, basically, is the theory that parts of a whole are in intimate interconnection, and as such that they cannot exist independently of the whole. Even this was not new. For centuries, ancient Chinese medicine, as well as that of the Indian Ayurveda, have treated the ill from a holistic view point. Traditional shamanic treatment included the physical as well as the psychological and spiritual spheres of the human condition. By this, Native Americans mean, mind, body, and spirit.

A key ingredient of the shamanic approach to healing, dating back to early humanity, is the belief that the health of the individual is inextricably connected to his or her surroundings. [And doesn't that have ramifications for today's world?] Consequently, the shaman works to promote harmony between the body, mind, and spirit as well as harmony within the community, the environment, and the Spirit World.

Earlier I noted there are at least four broad healing practices common to nearly all shaman. These practices include the use of herbal remedies, purging and or extraction, ceremonies of purification, and contacting the Spirit World. The shaman actually functions as an intermediary in the Spirit World, asking for answers to why a person is ill and what would make that person well again. Because there is a strong believe that all things in nature are connected and that there is a corresponding relationship to the Spirit World, the shaman accepts the notion spirits can help maintain, promote, and return one to good health.

Basically, these broad categories have been carried over into contemporary times. As with all procedures, there have been modifications. Today, for example, purging and extraction deal primarily with negative energy and negative entities. This is not the same as a religious exorcism.

Today's healers have many more issues with which to contend than did their earlier counterparts. Life styles have changed, foods have changed, chemical pollution and severe drug issues plague the modern shamanic healer's efforts.

HERBS AND THEIR USES

A knowledge of herbs and their uses is a given for the shaman in the treatment of his or her clients. Novices should not attempt herbal remedies. Individuals should not accept herbal remedies without checking with their medical practitioner.

One cannot expect to learn all the subtleties of herbals by using a book on herbal medicines, even though there are several excellent books available. We now have a Physician's Desk Reference for Herbal Medicine.

Never undertake the gathering of herbs and other plants in the wild without an expert guide with you. It is a dangerous activity. Many plants are poisonous and look similar to those that are not.

One plant leaf may closely resemble another, and it can be deadly. Tasting a leaf here and there is not acceptable behavior. Poison hemlock is often mistaken for wild parsnips or wild carrots. All parts of the hemlock are poisonous. The word hemlock actually comes from the Anglo-Saxon *hemieac*, which simply means 'shore plant'.

Berries of various plants are usable in the treatment of specific ailments. The shaman knows which berries are astringent, which can induce vomiting and those that can act as a laxative. Do not go off into the woods on a berry picking expedition unless you know which very specific berries are edible; not all blue berries can be consumed. The inkberry, for example, is poisonous.

The shaman uses herbs, plants, leaves, roots, and berries to make teas, salves, pastes, poultices, and rubs as well as for food to build body nutriments.

In today's modern scientific world, we forget that the plant kingdom is a vast reserve for healing and medicines. Fortunately, and that's a questionable assumption; we are changing. It is estimated that forty per cent of prescription drugs sold in the United States contain at least one ingredient derived from nature. Herbs encompass at least twenty-five per cent of all knows flowering plants, yet only about two per cent have been investigated for their medicinal use. [A concern here is the rape of the Rain Forest for plants and oil.]

Among the popular plants used by shaman for the treatment of ailments are Agrimony, American Mandrake, blue Lobelia, Cinquefoil, Dandelion, and Yarrow. Three mushrooms hold a current medical interest because of their support of the immune system and as cancer fighters. These are Lion's Mane, Reishi Mushrooms, and Chaga Mushrooms. None of these are poisonous.

For eons, certain herbs and plants have held a special place in human affairs. For example, herbals have been used in rituals, divination ceremonies, as spiritual cleansers, and in the treatment of those who suffer has been very common among shamanic cultures worldwide.

Over the centuries, a few herbs have enjoyed a long use and recognition. Among these are sweet grass, cedar, lemon grass, sage, Palo Santo, lavender, Kinnikinnick, Red Willow Bark, and miner's candlestick. All of these have been and are used in healing and purification ceremonies.

SHAMANIC HEALING AND SOUNDS

A shaman, as has been pointed out uses drums and rattles as part of his healing tools. He also makes use of his voice in chanting, often making repetitive sounds. The voice is one of the most common ways a shaman summons the Spirit World.

In the Native American cultures, specific songs are used for healing, and these very powerful songs are passed down from one generation of singers to the next. Each tribe has its own traditions and songs.

When one first hears a shaman's song, one can't help but feel the words are the same. Much of these may be due to the imitation in movies and television programs. The standard song appears to be "Ah Hey Ya" or perhaps something similar to "Ye Ha No Ha." A careful listening reveals the sounds are the vowel sounds of A, E, I, O, and U. During the chanting of these sounds; the sound of each vowel is elongated and is sung with a specific intent—the intent being to heal a client. Each vowel has its own meaning.

As tradition dictates, the four directions are acknowledged. The vowel A represents Earth and refers to the direction. North. E represents Air and the direction of East; the vowel I, represents Fire and the direction, South, O represents Water and the direction, West. The vowel sound of O represents the aether and significantly, it refers to being about; that is, existing. Once the four directions and the aether are recognized by the chanting shaman, the vowel sounds shift in their use and meaning. The vowel sound **A** is for purification while **I** emphasizes man's relationship to all things living and nonliving. **E** brings a connection to the Spirit World, and **U** takes the shaman into the Spirit's presence. O invokes the idea of innocence.

During his singing, the shaman may accompany himself with a drum eat or the beat of a rattle. He may use a helper for the drumming or shaking of the rattles. He may dance, in rhythm with the sounds, around the client.

Modern science has provided a better understanding of what the physical aspects of sound have on the human being. Simply, all things are vibrating molecules. When we are ill, those vibrations get out of sync. The shaman and his chanting, drums, and rattles connect to that vibration and realign the natural harmonics of the body; thus allowing it to heal itself.

PART FOUR
SHAMANIC ALTERED STATES

WHAT IS AN ALTERED STATE OF CONSCIOUSNESS?

Arnold M Ludwig is credited as the one who introduced the term *altered state of consciousness* in 1966. In 1969, Charles T. Tart published *Altered States of Consciousness: A Book of Readings*. It has been reported a "fully 90% of the world's cultures make use of one or more institutionalized altered state of consciousness, and in traditional societies, these are, almost without exception, sacred states.   [F4] The phrase, altered state of consciousness, has grown in world usage and reflects a wide variety of views as to what an altered state of consciousness is.

Simply put, when one loses a sense of identity with one's body, or for that matter, with a normal sense of perceptions, that individual is in an altered state of consciousness. Such individuals may experience a heightened sense of awareness. There is an attitude that what we call normal consciousness is not unitary, and that it is not necessarily being awake, and self-conscious.

A number of writers in the area of shamanism and altered states of consciousness talk about their use of mind-altering drugs. I make no apologies for my opposition to the use of hallucinogenic drugs. Elsewhere in this book I have made that point. With that said, how does one alter his or her state of consciousness? Specifically, what does the shaman do to journey to another realm?

To prepare for an altered state of consciousness, the shaman may fast for a couple of days; they may choose to go without sleep, and may even refuse water. An expectorant as well as a laxative may be used. I understand this may be done in some of areas of the

Amazon. The shaman may use smudging as a means to remove any negativity from his or her person. A sweat lodge may be used as a means of self-cleansing. Additionally, a shaman may spend time in quiet solitude.

There are many approaches a shaman may use to enter an altered state of consciousness. The use of sound, specifically the drum and rattle have already been mentioned. Another method of altering consciousness comes from the Far East. Meditation, especially deep meditation is a viable approach to transcending to another realm. In this instance, the shaman focuses on breathing, creating a specific rhythm by inhaling, holding, exhaling.

THE SHAMANIC TRANCE

Dr. Milton H. Erickson defines trance as an inner focus of attention. [F5] A trance state, necessary to have an altered state of consciousness, and to journey to the Spiritual World, is achievable through hypnosis. Self-hypnosis changes or alters the theta waves of the brain. Brainwave speed is measured in Hertz; that is, the number of cycles per minute. These, in turn, are divided into bands indicating slow, moderate, or fast waves.

Delta waves, usually .5 to 3 HZ, are the slowest and at the same time are the loudest of the brainwaves. These are generated in the very deepest meditation. At the Delta level, external awareness is suspended.

Theta waves, 3 to 8 HZ, dominate in deep meditation and act as a gateway to vivid imagery, intuition, and information beyond our normal conscious awareness.

Alpha waves, 8 to 12 HZ, operate during our quiet, pre-meditative thoughts.

Two of these play a significant role in the shamanic trance: Delta waves and Theta waves. Intoning the Delta waves begins the trance or Samadhi. The gateway to the altered state of consciousness or trance is enhanced by the increase in Theta waves.

During the self-induced trance, the shaman's spirit (soul) leaves the body and enters the world of the supernatural—to mind walk—seeking answers to his quest. This trance is non-focused per se. That is, the shaman's mind is open. He or she becomes a receptacle for information which flows until he or she receives a specific message related to the question. Once he or she has the message and acknowledges the messenger, he or she will come out of the trance and provide an interpretation.

In 1978 Joseph Bearwalker Wilson in a treatise provided an excellent discussion of a theory of trance. In his treatise, Wilson indicated the shaman enters a trance to fine-tune his senses and using those enhanced senses he can mind-travel the Spiritual World, to enter a different dimension.

THE STAGES OF SHAMANIC TRANCE

Of all the things a shaman does, the trance is most often the focus of discussion. It is, after all, the ultimate experience in shamanism. As I have said elsewhere, do not expect an immediate achievement of a trance state. You should not have the expectation that one lesson will take you to another level of reality. Practice makes perfect is the operative credo.

Generally speaking, there are four basic levels of shamanic trance. It is not my intent nor am I suggesting a shaman goes through each of these four levels each time he or she goes into a trance. Well, practiced shaman may go directly to the fourth level; thus, bypassing the other three.

The first level is more common among beginners. At this stage, the individual will have a sense of being physically relaxed, even drowsy. There is a tendency to stare off into space, unseeing and unhearing. During this time, the pulse rate slows down.

The second level produces a feeling that the whole body is heavy; a sense of detachment develops. Visual illusions may occur and there will be an awareness that you are in a trance state. It's not dissimilar to the feeling you have just before you go to sleep.

The third level brings a deep trance. Here you may actually choose a part of your body to remain pain free. There is greater sensitivity to temperature changes as well as atmospheric pressure. A loss of voluntary motion and reaction to external stimuli will occur.

In the fourth and final level of the shamanic trance, your eyes may be open and this will not cause any ill effect for the trance state. Control over several body functions such as heart beat, blood pressure, and body temperature becomes possible. There will be a recall of memories and even age regression may occur. There will be a feeling of lightness, of floating, or flying. Visual and auditory hallucinations are possible while in this fourth level of a trance.

The shaman who enters this fourth level travels into dreamtime or another dimension where he will receive his instruction. If the spirits are accommodating, the shaman's question will be given an answer.

Just because the shaman journeys to another dimension and communicates with those who abide there does not mean he will get the answers to his question(s). He may have to do some serious bargaining.

ECSTASY AND THE SHAMAN

**Figure 18 Hamatsa Emerging
from the woods**

Ecstasy may be defined as an emotional trance-like state in which an individual transcends normal consciousness. Involved is an expanded spiritual awareness during which time the shaman connects visually to the Spirit World.

Generally speaking, it is more profound than the normal trance created by the shaman to journey.

There are three areas of commonality in world shamanism and depending upon the culture, the emphasis on any one of these areas may differ. The first area common to all shamanic cultures is the recognition of a spiritual world peopled with spiritual entities. Second, there is worldwide agreement that there is a direct relationship between the Spiritual World and ordinary reality. The third area of commonality is that of ecstasy.

The three types of ecstasy are shamanic, prophetic, and mystical. Briefly, in prophetic ecstasy, the prophet speaks for the divine, whereas, in mystical ecstasy, the mystic comes into the presence of the divine reality. Our interest here, is the third type, shamanic ecstasy during which the shaman communes with those in the Spirit World to receive answers to his quest.

During this ecstatic trance, the shaman's soul leaves his physical body, ascends to the Upper World or descends to the Lower World to seek answers to his quest. Most likely, the shaman will experience all three perceptible levels of ecstasy; the physiological, psychological, and intuitive. The practiced shaman controls his trance and governs his return to the ordinary world.

CONSCIOUSNESS OF SPIRIT

Consciousness is a subjective experience. This means that you are aware of Self and of the world surrounding that Self. For the shaman, however, consciousness involves three elements: intentionality, selectivity, and continuity.

Intentionality means a Spirit Soma has deliberately decided to make contact. Selectivity refers to the choice-making processes the Spirit uses to select the shaman for a visit. Continuity relates to the ongoing processes involved in communication so that awareness is possible.

Awareness allows one to sense the presence of something else, that is, something more than. During these special moments, the shaman believes a spirit consciousness has made personal contact. Such a contact is an effort by the Spirit Soma to merge with human consciousness.

The purpose of this intentional merger is to transfer the Spirit Soma's essence to the shaman. During this process, the shaman may sense or actually visualize the presence of the Spirit Soma as a specific image such as that of a human face, or that of an animal.

A visit by a Spirit Soma requires recognition. Protocol demands such a recognition. A simple "welcome" is sufficient. Once a welcome is given, the shaman must wait to see if there is a message. The message may be verbal, image, or action. There is always the possibility that the Spirit Soma may be just making a probe to test the validity of the shaman's quest.

Fundamental to this shamanic notion of consciousness of spirit is the belief that all things are alive, that they have spirit, that is, they have Mana as

the indigenous islanders of the South Pacific call it—a
revered respect for the natural and non-ordinary worlds.

CREATING ALTERNATE REALITIES TODAY

Young mothers hum to their babies to quiet them down. Babies coo in a repetitive monotonous pattern to go to sleep. In today's world with its high pressured fast-paced life styles, psychoacoustics is very popular as a way to bring quietude to one's life.

Creating alternate realities using sound has a long, interesting, and varied history. Creating such realities is most noticeably true among the early peoples that populated the world. The serious practitioners were tribal shaman. Sound changes the opiate receptors of the brain and brings about a significant change in the subconscious.

The Internet is a riff with sound bites and longer pieces that claim to change your reality, to change the way you live, to transport you to another dimension. These sound bites increase the theta and beta waves in the brain. The subconscious mind is that part of the brain's activities of which we are not aware. It has powerful influence over one's actions and feelings. Sound activates this area within the brain. Ancient, as well as the modern shaman, prefers the sound of the drum.

At 200 to 225 beats per minute and in an unvaried pitch and tone, drumming is a most effective way to alter one's consciousness. Modern studies using electroencephalography demonstrate rhythmic drumming has a dramatic impact on the brain. With the sound alteration of brain waves, the shaman journeys to another dimension. Modern science, especially the proponents of String Theory, suggests there are at least ten, possibly eleven dimensions. Implications now suggest there is a twelfth and thirteenth dimension. The potential for journeying and connecting with spiritual entities is nearly limitless.

The novice to journeying may not realize transient migration or recognize he or she is in another dimension. Often, roadblocks prevent the move to another dimension. Among the most notable, roadblocks are external distractions of television, telephone, cell phone, barking dogs, noisy vehicles. Young children pose a distraction. To achieve a maximized effect one should have a quiet place, darkened, a CD player, or an iPod, and a set of earphones. There are a number of recordings of drumming available. Be selective. In listening to a binaural tape, CD, or mp3 file, and do not turn the volume up to its loudest level. A moderate level is recommended. The old saying of *if you don't succeed, try, try again* applies here.

Journeying or traveling into a different level (Lower World, Upper World, or to another dimension within these two worlds or even in the Middle World —Ordinary Reality)—is not the same as hallucinating. During a hallucination, one does not have control. In journeying, one does.

PART FIVE
SHAMAN AND SPIRIT AND SOUL

THE THREE S's IN SHAMANISM

Sixth century (BCE), Greek philosopher, Pythagoras, postulated each person is composed of three fundamental aspects: body, mind, and soul. Humans, instinctively inquisitive, have always been investigating and modifying the two worlds in which they normally exist—the physical and inner worlds.

Indigenous people around the world have a similar concept of the human being. No matter the claim, to the contrary, mankind is inexorably part of both worlds. It is this recognition that the shaman integrates into his world view and connects to the Spirit World.

For the shaman, the order in which the three fundamental aspects of the human being appear is significant. A body is required in order to have a place for the mind, and mind is a perquisite for the soul. The implication is the body is a receptacle. We are a soul with a body!

Generally, we speak of a human physical being as an entity with a soul or spirit and a self. In the shaman's view humans, animals, plants, rocks, wind, rain, sun, stars, moon, and water are alive with Spirits. Unfortunately, modern man has a somewhat inaccurate image of spirit, that it is a ghostly apparition with lots of moaning and groaning or the rattling sounds during a séance that is designed to communicate with the dead. Nothing could be further from the truth.

Perhaps a better word for spirit would be *essences*, meaning that which makes a person human, a tree a tree, an eagle, and eagle. Aristotle's "substances" are not an equivalent, nor are Plato's "pure forms." The shamanic concept of Spirit is closer to that of the Ancient Egyptian notion of BA, which many translate as "soul" or "spiritual manifestation."

From a practical viewpoint, spirit is that which makes a thing what it is. It's the *noumenon*. Spirit consciousness, as a consequence of the notion of death, has a problem when death is viewed as the final arbitrator. If, however, death is a rebirth into another life, much as a child from its mother's womb emerges into another world, then spirit consciousness as Spirit-Soul is viable.

Even though Spirit and Soul are essential to a shaman and the cohesiveness they provide, there is no denial of the various categories or of other forces or qualities. The shaman accepts them all; He denies nothing.

Concern with the nature of the Self develops because of our inherent need to experience authenticity. We have to know who we are. This drive to know who we are, often causes issues and these manifest as psychological malfunctions. This is particularly true when we forget there is a singularity when it comes to the Self. The three aspects of the human being function as a single unit.

The shaman has a primary concern with divisive nature because he views it as a cause of body and psychological illness. The healing ceremonies of the shaman are done to determine if a part of the soul has been snatched from the ill person, if the soul has been damaged, or if it has been removed. Once the condition has been identified, the shaman may do an extraction, may go into a trance state during which time he solicits the help of the Spirit World to find, retrieve, and return that soul or missing part to his client.

SHAMANISM AND TIME

Greek Sophist, Antiphon, claimed time was not a reality, but a concept. Philosopher, Parmenides maintained time was an illusion. Time is accepted as a dimension during which present, past, and future events occur. Later philosophers Leibniz and Kant held time to be neither an event nor a thing, and that it is unto itself and is immeasurable. Further, they believed time could not be traveled. For some, time has a subjective element; that is, one feels it as a sensation or an experience. However, in today's world, science has demonstrated time travel is possible on the molecular level by teleporting an atom. This is quantum entanglement.

Whatever the viewpoints, it is agreed that we have time in a void. There would be nothing to which it could be related. It would not exist. To understand time, it must connect to something. Time is a form of perception and for the shaman, that's all time is—a perception of three divisions, present, past, and future. Time is not a ticking clock nor is it the day-week-month time. It simply is, and the shaman moves in and out of these divisions depending upon the need and the world to which he wishes to migrate.

During the altered state of consciousness (trance), the shaman is oblivious of all time. He, frequently with his animal helper, is concentrating on finding the answer to a health issue for a client. Depending upon the need, the shaman may go to the Upper World or the Lower World. If, during his altered state, he senses the answer lies within the Middle World (the world in which he normally lives,) he will seek help from the spirit dwelling there.

The shaman's movement into other realms is non-ordinary reality or parallel universes. And in those, time, all time, flows seamlessly. It is never linear. It is simultaneous. This gives the impression that a shaman is here and there at the same time. And he is!

SPIRIT HELPERS

The shaman's goal is to connect human consciousness to the natural and spiritual world. To do this, he or she uses animal and plant totems. Briefly, a totem is a symbol representing a spiritual aspect of an animal or plant and has importance to an individual or group. The shaman, as noted, connects to the spirit of the animal or plant through subliminal trance. The shaman may take one of these helpers with him as he seeks answers to his quest.

How does one acquire a spirit animal or plant? There are a variety of methods. Often, the spirit animal or plant will come to the person while he or she is on a vision quest. The spirit animal's purpose and function are to help or guide the shaman.

Can a non-shaman have a spirit animal or plant? Most human beings can have an animal or plant spirit. There are various ways of acquiring one. Foremost, and before selection actually begins, you should have some idea as to why you want a spirit helper or guide and second; you should have a clear idea of what you expect of the helper. Can you have more than one spirit helper? Yes.

Once you have answered the two questions posed above, sit quietly and still in an outdoor area. Observe the area around you. Notice the animal, plant, and insect life. Pay close attention to their characteristics. Zero in on any that holds a fascination for you. If your focus is a plant, examine its leaves, stem, and flower if it has one. Smell the plant. Notice texture, sheen, and if there are gradations of color. Are the leaves elongated, round, pear-shaped, smooth edges or jagged edges? Don't pick it!

If your attention is drawn to a bird, squirrel, rabbit, chipmunk, or deer that comes into your vision zone, don't offer food. You may do that only after you have selected an animal if you are not in violation of laws governing wild animals in your area. The objective is not to make them a pet.

If the plant or animal continues to hold your fascination ask yourself which of its qualities or characteristics have the most interest for you. Once you have noted that information, decide if you have the same qualities or some of them. Does the plant or animal really reflect qualities you would like to have? If so, then you most likely have selected your power animal or plant.

Can an animal select you? Absolutely. You will know that by recurring experiences with that animal. Some may call this synchronicity. Among Native Americans and some of the indigenous tribes of the Amazon, it is most significant if an animal spirit chooses you. It is very powerful and most likely will be a life-long spirit guide. Several years ago, a friend, stepped out into his yard and as he was enjoying the morning sunrise a seagull fell from the sky and hit the ground just a couple of feet from where he was standing. The next day another seagull arrived and it continued to stay for several days. My friend said the seagull was his spirit guide.

There are three types of spirit guides or helpers. The first, mentioned above, is the life-long spirit guide. This tutelary will work with you throughout your earth-life. Journey Spirit Guide is the second type of helper. This one may stay a short time, or it may remain for an extended period of time. It depends upon how long it takes you to follow the way given to you by the guide. Time signifies the difference between this second type of spirit guide and the third type. The third type is the message guide. This one brings you an important and often life-altering message. At some point, if you tune into the magic of spirit animals and plants, you may very well experience all three types of spirit helpers.

Can you have more than one spirit guide or helper? Yes, you can and each one may serve a different purpose or function.

THE SHAMAN AND SOUL LOSS

In psychology, the loss of one's normal integration of conscious functioning is a dissociation. However, for the shaman, this is the loss of soul or a part of the soul. Whenever a person loses his soul or part of it, his physical being reflects that loss. This loss may be shown as a feeling of a lack luster daily existence, that is a lack of a personal dynamism. There are several indicators of soul loss. Chief among these are chronic illness, feeling emotionally empty, depressed, lapses in memory, and in some cases, a sense of dying.

The soul may leave a person because of an abusive situation—either sexual, physical, or emotional. A person (a parent or spouse, an intimate friend)may be fearful of losing an individual (a child, husband, wife, a parent, best friend), sometimes will take a part of that individual's soul. By doing so, the thief is operating under the assumption that he or she and the loved one will always be together. A soul snatcher may do so because he or she believes they will acquire that soul's energy. Of course, for whatever reason, an evil spirit may snatch the soul.

In the event, the soul's development stagnates; that is, if it goes over to the dark side, or if an entity steals it, and it can't find its way back, the soul may become irreversibly corrupted. If it is lost, it may actually experience annihilation, that is, a depletion of its energy. As a consequence of such depletion, the soul may wander aimlessly throughout the cosmos.

The inactivation of the soul results in the erasure of the individual's personality; that is, it has dissociation. The *I of the I-Am* dissolves. It then returns to its source of creation, the Akasha. It is as though it had never existed. If that happens, the physical body dies.

If the activation of the soul does not take place, it cannot enter one's conscious reality; thus, we can say, one has lost his soul.

Because the shaman believes soul loss is the cause of many ills, he is concerned about the depletion of one's spiritual energy. That depletion becomes all the more serious if the soul permanently leaves the body. If that happens, the body, as indicated dies. The primary goal of the shaman is to retrieve the lost part(s) of the soul or the entire soul in order to return the person to natural harmony, balance, and physical zest.

Parts of the soul that leaves the body on their own accord don't go to a soul repository and remain in limbo. They continue to live a parallel existence in non-ordinary realms of reality. The shaman, using an altered state of consciousness, travels to these realms to find the soul or soul parts and return it to the sick person.

In summary, there are three main causes for soul loss, an individual has suffered a trauma, experienced a sense of abandonment, or the soul has been stolen.

Ake Hulkranz [F6] draws a distinction between soul loss and spirit power loss. Soul loss refers to the disappearance of a soul to a place from which it cannot return on its own volition. Spirit power loss refers to a Spirit that is so intimately and strongly connected to and with an individual that his or her life is in grave danger.

RETRIEVING THE SOUL

The 40,000-year-old practice which we call shamanism has as one of its fundamental beliefs the notion that one's soul or part of that soul may leave the body because of disease, by being stolen, or by being given away.

The soul may be stolen by a spirit who feels it has been wronged, or because it is evil. It seems strange to suggest one would give away a part of one's soul. A mother may do that for a lost child or a gravely ill child or a spouse may do that. In dealing with the client, the shaman tries to determine which case it may be: stolen, given away, or has left the body because of another illness.

The client is surrounded with healing herbs, stones (crystals), and is smudged with sage or Palo Santo or a combination.

Altering his state of consciousness is necessary so the shaman can journey to another realm. He or she may sit down during this alteration, or he may stand in a suspended state of movement. In going to the Spirit World, the shaman takes with him his Spirit Animal or Spirit Guide (this may be the soul of an ancestor) who finds the soul and directs the shaman to that location. Once the soul or its part is located, the shaman begins the negotiations for its return. This endeavor is fought with danger for both the shaman and the client. As a cautionary measure, the shaman does not use his own powers to retrieve the soul. Any such attempt could result in suffering a depletion of his powers, skills, energy and could bring about his physical death.

If he is successful in the negotiations, the shaman returns to the present world and then literally blows the soul or its part back into the client's body. Usually, this is at the top of the head or into the client's open mouth.

Is the shaman always successful? No, success is not guaranteed. Sometimes, the client is so ill or broken hearted; he or she chooses not to survive.

Today much is being written about shamanic soul retrieval as psychological counseling. The shift from shamanic soul retrieval to psychological disassociation, depression, anxiety, sadness, low self-esteem, and or anger is a disservice. Caution needs to be the operative in such cases. A shaman is so much more than a psychologist and to name modern psychological practices as shamanic is equally a disservice.

PART SIX
THE SHAMANIC WORLD VIEW

THE SHAMAN'S WORLD VIEW

Figure 19 Slow Bull Medicine Man

When one thinks of a *world view,* some grandiose scheme of things floods one's mind. And in this instance, the term *world view* is most likely to be too narrow to describe how a shaman views things since he or she appears to have no limitations. A belief system may be a more appropriate phrase.

First, among the major tenets of the shamanic belief system is the lack of a need to confirm the world. For the shaman, what is, is. One cannot prove or disprove a perception. Perceptions are totally internalized and personal. Be mindful; however, one may change one's perceptions, and a shaman never hesitates to change his if it is necessary.

Second, the shaman believes the Self, and all else are connected, moving together in fluidity just as are mind and matter are irrevocably intertwined. The fundamental basis for this second tenet is the notion that all things contain a life-force, a soul, or a spirit. This includes human beings, all animals, and plants. It also includes rivers, streams, lakes, oceans, mountains, the winds, and the planetary system. Because the shaman accepts all of these as his potential helpers, he renders respect to all of them. His prayers demonstrate that respect.

The third aspect of the shamanic belief system is the notion that the individual is fundamentally responsible for his own health. One's health is the creation of that individual. This is significant since the shaman functions, primarily, as a healer. The key here is creation. The shaman's job is to determine the cause for the malfunction of that creation.

How the shaman views reality is the fourth tenet of the shamanic belief system. For the shaman, reality is not just a physical representation. Both ordinary and non-ordinary realities exist in the shaman's view. The practiced shaman is comfortable in either reality. All realities are possible. If they are not, that places a limit on creation. Peggy Malanti writes, "......reality is perceived as being layered rather than flat and single-dimensional." She continues, "Existence is not only perceived as being layered in parallel and overlapping horizontal dimensions, but it is also layered vertically." [F7] Modern physics supports this through the concept of parallel universes.

The fifth principle involved in the shaman's world view is that the world, the universe, the cosmos is a living, changing, evolving entity. It is alive and the shaman, in turn, flows with whatever those changes may be.

The following statement probably bests represents shamanic identity: "I am that I am and the World is as I dream it."

The shaman's view is certainly substantiated by modern science. Today we know that all things are made of molecules, and these are in a state of constant movement. Movement, for the shaman, is indicative of a life force; thus all things are alive.

THE SHAMANIC REALMS

The traditional shaman believes there are three accessible realms to which he can travel. These are commonly called Upper, Middle, and Lower realms. At the outset, each is distinctive and each is accessed in a different way. Kenneth Meadows lists four levels. He divides the Lower Realm into two parts; the second, he calls the "under world." [F8] He does not equate this with the religious concept of Hell. For the shaman, Hell does not exist as it is described in the Judeo-Christian religious literature. Because I have concerns about the way the Lower Realm is presented in some of the contemporary literature about shamanism, I first will discuss the Lower Realm.

In Ancient Greek literature, there is the story of Persephone and Demeter and there are multiple versions of this story. Briefly, Hades takes Persephone. Finally, a deal is brokered for her return to the world. Demeter has her daughter in tow and is warned not to look back. She does, and Persephone is lost to the underworld. The point is simple. In the Lower Realm, there is a protocol that is to be followed. If it is violated dire consequences result, that is, one may not return to the Middle World. An even older story, that of Enkidu in the Sumerian myth of Gilgamesh, Enkidu is sentenced to death by the Gods as punishment for taking part in the killing of Humbaba and the Bull of Heaven. The distraught Gilgamesh journeys to the Lower World and because he did not follow correct protocol, Enkidu is denied re-entrance into the world.

Some of the current shamanic literature paints the Lower Realm as a place to meet lovely animals, spirits of the deceased and even prehistoric creatures such as the fabled Unicorn. This is totally misleading, and dangerous, especially for the novice.

The Lower Realm is composed of a variety of spirits, some of whom may be evil. [F9] If one doesn't enter this realm with respect and a question limited to a single issue, one risks the same fate as that of Enkidu. In shamanic terms, the shaman loses his soul and life.

A shaman enters the Lower Realm during a trance state; that is, in an altered state of consciousness. Usually, the entrance to the Lower Realm which is located in the bowels of the earth is through an opening in a tree trunk, or a cave. Whatever the starting point, it is to that place the shaman returns. Remember; don't go with a chorus of questions. Keep your issue focused.

The Middle Realm, the realm in which we currently exist and is often called "Ordinary Reality" also has spirits. Evelyn C Rysdyk, in discussing this realm, says it is the place of animal spirits and those spirits that are beyond our ordinary experience and the shaman must have a clear relationship here. She says, "This is critical because this is also the place of *manifestations*, that is, where the formless spiritual energies develop physicality or become embedded." [F10] I believe these spirits are the souls of deceased bodies who most likely have more to learn or have assignments to be completed. They are accessible to the shaman and can offer help with his question and or in healing a client. I prefer to think of this as a parallel universe. [F11] In a parallel universe, things will look and feel much the same as they do in ordinary reality. There will be some differences; for example, colors, light, and sounds may take on a gossamer-like quality. One may experience fluctuations not dissimilar to when the lights in one's home flicker. Because human as are all things made of vibrating atoms, the shaman has to tune into those vibrations as he moves about in the Middle Realm. To change something in this parallel universe to bring about a positive impact on the world of ordinary time, the shaman changes his vibrational level.

In terms of garnering reliable information to help his client, the Middle Realm is generally visited first. If an answer or suggested solution is not acquired there, the shaman moves to the Upper Realm.

Once a trance state is achieved and an alternate state of consciousness is fully developed, the shaman may then choose to move to the Upper Realm. It is there the shaman seeks his spirit teacher or an available spirit that will actively participate with him in bringing back a stolen, lost, or part of a soul, or develop an answer to his question. The Upper Realm is populated by with spirits that may take the shape of an animal, an obscure abstract shape, a human head, or a full-bodied human. As with the other realms, good manners are a prerequisite. Acknowledge the spirit when it makes is presence known, and thank it for seeing you. In other words, express an appreciation.

There is debate over protocol. Should one ask the spirit for help or state the need? Two examples will illustrate the issue. In the first example, the shaman says, "I ask that you help me heal my client." In the second example, the shaman says, "Help me heal my client." I caution you not to use an abrasive tone.

Does a shaman ever ask for personal help? Of course, seeking the Spirit World to help heal him is completely within his prerogative. He can ask for personal guidance, cleansing, protection, and a host of other things.

Can a shaman tell the future and change future events? The shaman within my experience do not view themselves as psychics. One, who trained and lived in the Amazon for eleven years does not view himself as a healer but rather as a bringer of messages and those are future related to the whole world and not to an individual. Another shaman, trained by the Tibetan shaman, views herself not as a prophet nor as a healer, but, as one who reveals colors and auras in individuals. However, another, who has traveled the world studying shamanic ways, prefers to be viewed as a shamanic practitioner rather than as a shaman. She feels that title belongs only to aboriginal peoples. A shaman will not tell a person he or she is going to win the lotto. Don't even bother to ask.

PART SEVEN
ON BECOMING

HOW ONE BECOMES A SHAMAN

Figure 20 Navajo Shaman

A check on the Internet will bring up several courses related to becoming a shaman. These are offered through retreats, colleges, and universities and provide certification. These programs offer ways to learn basic shamanic healing, energy healing, earth-based spirituality, shamanic journeying, how to awaken one's spiritual abilities, gain soul knowledge, learn shamanic wisdom through mask making, and learn how to enter non-ordinary reality for healing. Does one become a shaman by taking a college course, a seminar, or a retreat? My answer is a resounding no!

How then, does one become a shaman? I do not consider a shamanic practitioner as a shaman nor am I implying those who are practitioners are of any less value. Those practioners whom I know do not call themselves shaman.

How then does one become a shaman? There are seven ways one may become a shaman.

First, one may inherit shamanic power, knowledge, and skills from a family member who is a shaman. This "passing on" involves the teaching of the novice the secrets of the trade. One of my former college students was a shaman in training. He was being trained by his grandmother, and his training had begun was he was four years old. He hoped to be admitted to the tribe as a shaman when he was in his twenties.

Second, a person who suffers a life-threatening illness and

experiences a miraculous recovery may be able to pass on the healing experience he or she went through. If so, the individual is a shaman. The proof in the pudding, so to speak, is if a person receiving the attention of this previously ill person becomes well.

Third, a child who shows special gifts for seeing, for traveling, or for healing is given particular attention—watched for further signs marking him or her as significantly different from other children. When the child reaches adulthood, a current shaman will test him. If the young adult is successful during the testing, then he or she is accepted as a shaman.

Fourth, a person may pay for training. The teacher is a shaman and agrees to teach the healing ways, including special ceremonies, and the use of healing herbs. The important point here is that one engages a bona fied shaman. This is generally costly and will take a long period of time. Do not expect an overnight or weekend experience. Unfortunately, one of the things happening with the increased interest in shamanism is the rise in pseudo-shamanism in some of the South American countries and in Sibera where there have been recurring efforts to unionize the shaman.

Fifth, one is visited by a spirit who imparts certain knowledge. The help of a shaman is necessary to guide the person in understanding the spirit messages. Essential in this approach, the individual must be open to receiving spirit visitations. A shaman is required to help the individual ask the right questions of the spirit visitor and to interpret meaning.

Sixth, the individual goes into isolation for three or four days. In our current age, it may be an isolation chamber, a deprivation chamber, a cave, a pop-up tent, or anything else that would provide absolute quiet and darkness. During this time, the individual takes no food or water. This is the traditional "vision quest." During this period of isolation, a spirit may make itself known and reveal a life-path to be followed. This path is not always that of a shaman. Such an undertaking should never be taken lightly and should always be with a trained person's guidance. One's personal health and phyiscal conditon are prime concerns. Prolonged isolation may have extended negative effects.

Seventh, one goes into an altered state of consciousness. This may be drug induced or through auditory means such as drumming, rattles, or any of the modern binaural recordings that are available. During this state, the individual goes through body dismemberment. Whether hallucinogens or sound is used to go into the altered state of consciousness, a human guide should be available during this move into an altered state of consciousness.

As a cautionary note, remember the mind is a delicate, sensitive, and still mysterious part of the human being. Much is known about the brain, but the mind is entirely something different. It can be easily abused or destroyed. The journey to become a shaman is not for the light of heart nor is it a game for the weekend warrior.

THE VISION QUEST

The term vision quest has two popular uses; initiation of a young person into adult society, and as part of the initiation of one as a shaman.

Several factors emerge when considering the traditional vision quest. Hardship is necessary, and it is based on the notion that there are certain experiences essential to having dreams and or vision quests. These hardships include social isolation, fasting, water deprivation, exhausting physical exercise to create fatigue and nonstop singing of a monotonous song or the continual repetition of a prayer.

A shamanic vision quest may include staying in a cave for three or four nights without food, water, or light, staying in a sheltered, or isolated wooded area without benefit of cover. In both, sleep is deprived. The candidate must force himself or herself to stay awake. This may cause one to hallucinate.

Hyperventilation and exposing oneself to extreme temperatures and in rare instances, subjection to self-inflicted pain in some cases may produce a vision. I do not recommend either of these approaches because of their inherent danger. Extreme hyperventilation can result in cardiac arrest and potential death. Self-inflicted pain usually includes piercing and cutting, which can lead to serious life-threatening infections.

Medicine Grizzlybear Lake (Bobby Lake-Thom) says, "it is through the vision quest that we get our power. Through a vision quest, we can discover who we really are." [F12] He points out the difference between a dream and a vision. Basically, dreams are fleeting and short lived. Often just a few seconds. Furthermore, they are often confusing and easily forgotten. A vision is longer in duration and is vividly clear. It is many times very dynamic. One does not forget a vision.

The vision quest, as mentioned previously, is used by the shaman to seek advice. Lake says, "dreams are the doorway to the spirit world; a vision is the spirit world." [F13] This is a significant differentiation. In the spirit world, the shaman can and does interact with the spirits he or she encounters there. The shaman is in control; whereas, in a dream (unless it is what is called a lucid dream), such control does not exist. As an aside, there are herbs that help lucid dreaming. Two come to mind: Mugwort and Ghost Pipe.

SHAMAN, CRYSTALS, AND STONES

In keeping with the shamanic belief that all things are alive, it is to be expected crystals and stones would be used in their shamanic healing processes. A crystal or stone is a vibrating mass of atoms as are all substances, including animal life. Crystals are formed within the earth or in outer space (Moldavite) and have taken thousands of years to form. Crystals and healing stones have been found at ancient burial sites. Fore example, crystals, specifically quartz crystals, have been found in 8,000-year-old burial sites in California. Crystal power, like those of the Spirit World, is not to be lightly taken.

Crystals have the power of amplification, and transformation was well as physical and emotional healing. Joti Gore says there are "two principles when working with crystals, meditation and respect." [F14] One doesn't just pick p a crystal and say heal. It doesn't work that way. A shaman has carefully selected the crystals he uses. He has held them in his hands, sensed their energy or lack thereof. He has felt their vibrations. He has chosen a crystal based on his intent; that is, what the reason is for considering it. He most likely has meditated prior to his selection

The crystals are cleansed before being applied and are cleansed after each use. Crystals are then programmed for their specific use. Once issues have been identified, the client may have crystals and other healing stones placed around his or her body. They may be placed on the body. Generally, if the stones are heated, they are placed around the body and lain on a variety of wet herbs. The steam created in this way is smudged over the client's body

During the placement of the crystals or stones, the shaman may chant a prayer in which he asks for the crystals to use their power and energy to help heal his client. Crystal Healer, Ashley Dalke says, "crystal healing is a form of vibrational medicine in which subtle energy given off by a crystal is used to treat the body." [F15]

Different crystals have unique purposes and use. Michael Harner says, "while there is potentially an almost infinite variety of power objects, there is one particular kind that is regularly found in the keeping of shamans. This is the quartz crystal."[F16] Goldstone, for example, is sued to relieve stomach stress and Labradorite is used for healing old memories, including past-life issues. In this situation, the shaman travels to another real to seek what the past-life issues are. Ocean Jasper is excellent to use for restorative tissue deterioration of internal organs. As with the use of herbals, it is always best to consult your doctor before trying any of these treatments. Check for allergies, for example. Please note the books on crystals included in the bibliography.

ADDENDUM

The following photographs are from the family album. They are included here for those who might be curious. The first is a photo of the author at age seven sitting on the rock that played a significant role in his vision quest. The second photo is of the log cabin in which he spent every summer for fourteen years. The third photo is of the cousins Jean Skipper and Lenora Lightwater(questions remain about this photo) and the fourth is the author's life-line created by shaman L. Black.

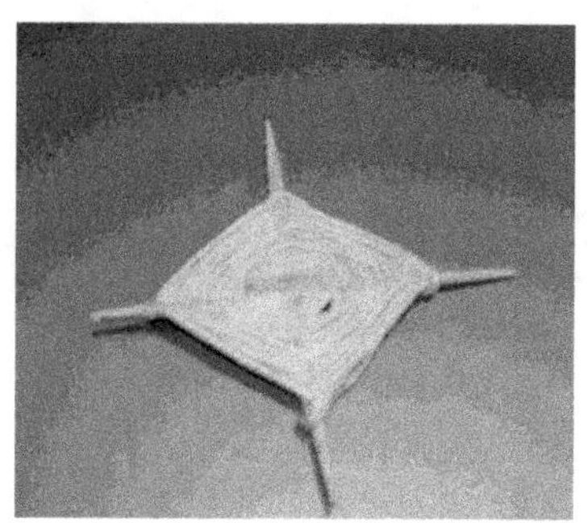

PART EIGHT
BIBLIOGRAPHIES

BOOKS ON SHAMANISM

Andrews, Ted. Animal Speak The Spiritual and Magical Powers of Creatures Great and Small. St. Paul. Llewellyn Publications. 2004.

Drury, Nevil. Shamanism. Shaftesbury. Element. 1996.

Eliade, Mircea. Shamanism: Archaic Techniques of Ecstasy. London. Arkana. 1989.

Freke, Timothy. Shamanic Wisdom Keepers. New York. Godsfield Book. 1999

Harner, Michael. Hallucinogens & Shamanism. London. Oxford University Press. 1973.

Harner, Michael. The Way of the Shaman. Tenth Anniversary Edition.SanFrancisco. Harper. 1990.

Harner, Michael. Cave and Cosmos. Berkley. North Atlantic Books. 2013.

Ingerman, Sandra and Hank Wesselman. Awakening the Spirit World. The Shamanic Path of Direct Revelation. Boulder. Sounds True. 2000.

Kalweit, Holger. Dreamtime & Inner Peace. The World of the Shaman. Boston. Shambhala. 1988.

Kalweit, Holger. Shamans, Healers and Medicine Men. Boston. Shambhala. 1992.

Versluis, Arthur. Native American Traditions. Shaftesbury. Element. 2001.

Villoldo, Alberto. Shaman, Healer, Sage. New York. Harmony Books. 2000.

Walter, Mariko Namba and Eva Jane Neumann Friedman (eds). Shamanism An Encyclopedia of World Beliefs, Practices, and Culture, Vol 1 and II, Santa Barbara. ABC CLIO. 2004.

Wesselman, Hank. Spiritwalker. Messages from the Future. New York. Bantam.1995.

Wesselman, Hank and Jill Kuykendall. Spirit Medicine, Healing in the Sacred Realms. Carlsbad, CA. Hay House, Inc. 2004.

Wood, Nicholas. The Book of Shaman. Happauge. Barron. 2001.

BOOKS ON CRYSTALS

Lembo, Margaret Ann. The Essential Guide to Crystals, Minerals and Stones.Woodbury. Llewellyn Worldwide. 2013.

Melody. Love is in the Earth A Kaleidoscope of Crystals Updated. Wheat Ridge, CO. Earth-Love Publishing House. 1995

Raphaell, Katrina. Crystal Enlightment The Transforming Properties of Crystals and Healing Stones. Santa Fe. Aurora Press. 1995.

Raphaell, Katrina. Crystal Healing The Therapeutic Application of Crystals and Stones. Santa Fe. Aurora Press. 1987.

Raphaell, Katrina. The Crystalline transformation A synthesis of Light. Santa Fe. Aurora Press. 1990.

Simmons, Robert. Stones of the New Consciousness Healing, Awakening & Co-creating with Crystals, Minerals, & Gems. East Montpellier. Heaven & Earth Publishing LLC. North Atlantic Books. Berkeley. 2009.

BOOKS ON HERBS AND MEDICINALS

Berk, Sally Ann. The Herb Guide. New York. Black Dog and Leventhal. 2001.

Cunningham, Scott. Cunningham's Encyclopedia of Magical Herbs. (Reprint)Woodbury. Llewellyn Publications. 2005.

Foster, Stephen and James A. Duke. Eastern Central Medicinal Plants and Herbs. Boston. Houghton Mifflin Company. 2000.

Hutchens, Alma R. Indian Herbalogy of North America. Boston. Shambhala. 1991.

Hutchens, Alma r. A Handbook of Native American Herbs. Boston. Shambhala. 1992.

Jaenicke, Christof (ed). PDR for Herbal Medicine, 4th Edition. New York. Thomson Reuters Publishers. 2007.

Kane Charles W. Herbal Medicine. Trends and Traditions. Lincoln. Lincoln Town Press. 2009.

Pojar, Jim and Andy MacKinnon. Plants of the Pacific Northwest Coast. Redmond. Lone Pine. 1994.

Tilford, Gregory L. Edi ble and Medicinal Plants of the West. Missoula. Mountain Press Publishing. 1997.

LIST OF ILLUSTRATIONS

14. Palo Santo stick. Wilson, Suzanne V. 2018. Private Collection
15. Sage Bundle. Wilson, Suzanne V. 2010. Private Collection
16. Shaman's Staff. Hand carved Crow Talking Stick by William Paulson, 2010. Wilson, Suzanne V. 2014. Private Collection
17. Sia Buffalo Dancer. Curtis, Edward S. 1926. Call number lot 12316-C. Library of Congress Collection
18. Hamatsa Emerging from the Woods. Curtis, Edward S. 1914. Call number lot 12328-A. Library of Congress Collection
19. Slow Bull Medicine Man. Curtis, Edward S. 1907. Call number Illus in E77 C97ac-Rare Books. Library of Congress Collection
20. Navajo Shaman. Hillers, John K. 1872. Call number lot 12775(H). Library of Congress Collection

ALSO BY NORMAN W. WILSON

<u>Textbooks:</u>

Butterflies and all that Jazz with Drs. James G. Massey and James A. Powell

Windows and Images: An Introduction to the Humanities with Drs. James G. Massey and James A. Powell

The Humanities: Contemporary Images

<u>Nonfiction:</u>

So You THINK You want to be a Buddhist?

Promethean Necessity and Its Implications for Society

DUH! The American Educational Disaster

The Sayings of Esaugetuh: The Master of Breath

A Shaman's Journey Revealed Through Poetry with Gavriel Navaro

How to Make Moral and Ethical Decisions: A Guide

How to GET What You Really WANT

Healing- The Shaman's Way

Activating Your Spirit Guides

Shamanic Manifesting

<u>Fiction:</u>

The Shaman's Quest

The Shaman's Transformation

The Shaman's War

The Shaman's Genesis

The Shaman's Revelation

The Making of a Shaman

FOOTNOTES

[F1] www.spirittalk.net/native-american-about.html

[F2] Photo from Wikimedia. Commons usage.

[F3] The author makes no claim as to the accuracy or benefit of drumming to reduce aches, pains, or any other physical or psychological illness. He has only his own experiences to rely upon. His experience with a drummer lead to a shamanic journey.

[F4] B.B. Walsh in Textbook of Transpersonal Psychiatry and Psychology (Kindle Edition), B. Scotton, A. Chinen, and J. Battista, Eds. 2009. In the 1996 edition, p. 101.

[F5] Milton H. Erickson (1901-1980) was an American psychiatrist who specialized in medical hypnosis.

[F6] Hulkranz, Ake. Conceptions of the Soul Among North American Indians: A Study in religious ethnology. The Ethnographical Museum, Monograph Series, Publication No. 1 .Stockholm. Caslon Press. 1953

[F7] Malanti, Peggy. "The Shamanic View of the World" in Walksoftly2's Blog. 2011.

[F8] Meadows, Kenneth. The Shamanic Experience: A Practical Guide to Psychic Powers. Rochester, VT. Bear and Company, 2003.

[F9] An evil spirit is a soul that has used up its life-force by doing bad things.

[F10] Rysdyk, Evelyn C. Spirit Walking A Course in Shamanic Power. San Francisco. Weiser Books. 2013

[F11] Wilson, Norman W. The Shaman's Transformation. Camano Island, WA. Mélange

Publishing, 2011 for a description of parallel universe experience.

[F12] Lake, Medicine Grizlybear. Native Healer Initiation into an Ancient Art. Wheaton, Ill. Quest Books, 1991, p. 41.

[F13] Ibid. p. 43.

[F14] From www.nakedshaman.com. 2013.

[F15] The Shaman's Well. The Basis of Crystal Healing. 2011.

[F16] Harner, Michael. The Way of the Shaman. Tenth Anniversary Edition. San Francisco. Harper. 1990. P. 109.